GRADE ONE ENGLISH

Practice for Grade One

Packed with English activities!

SYNONYMS
HOMONYMS
GRAMMAR
GAMES

I am red.
You can eat me.
I am a fruit.

I am a _____.

I am a safari animal.
I look like a horse.
I am black and white.

I am a _____.

I can swim.
I have gills.

I am a _____.

I live o____
I have wo____

I am a _____

Designed by Flowerpot Press
www.FlowerpotPress.com
PAB-0811-0164
ISBN: 978-1-4867-1480-3
Made in U.S.A/Fabriqué aux États-Unis

TABLE OF CONTENTS

The Great Canadian Workbook series from Flowerpot Press was developed with your child's success and enjoyment in mind. The activities are carefully organized to progress in a logical manner, but also varied to keep children motivated and entertained. The series is sure to appeal to the needs of all children, whether they need some extra practice or want a chance to work ahead. The journey through an individual workbook is easy to follow, and the content and complexity of each level builds on the previous workbook and flows naturally into the next.

Grade One English is the fourth English workbook in the series. It is ideal for children who can read and write simple sentences with assistance. Your child will begin with fun phonics activities, and by the end of the workbook they will be able to identify parts of speech, form plural nouns, differentiate between related words, and read and respond to a variety of reading comprehension activities.

The learning adventure doesn't end here. Continue to develop your child's skills and love of learning with other workbooks in the Great Canadian Workbook series:

Determine whether the word begins with a vowel or consonant. Draw a line from the pictures to the correct box.

VOWEL

CONSONANT

Say the name of each picture and draw a line to match the pictures to the correct beginning consonants.

Learning Goal: Review consonants and match pictures to the correct beginning letters.

6

Say the name of each picture and draw a line to match the pictures to the correct beginning consonants.

K

L

M

N

P

Q

R

Learning Goal: Review consonants and match pictures to the correct beginning letters.

Say the name of each picture and draw a line to match the pictures to the correct beginning consonants.

S

T

W

V

X

Y

Z

Learning Goal: Review consonants and match pictures to the correct beginning letters.

Say the name of the picture and write the ending sound. The first one is done for you.

G

M

N

Learning Goal: Review consonants and word endings.

10

Circle the beginning consonant for each picture.

p   l   k   c

k   p   l   s

l   h   k   p

h   p   k   c

Say the name of the picture and write the beginning sound. The first one is done for you.

Learning Goal: Review consonants and word beginnings..

Colour the balloons with words that end in consonants.

apple
fish
jersey
helmet
wolf
ox
deer
bear
lake
goose
skate
antler
play
go
hat
what
near
please
look
talk
see
leaf
ski
smile
tent
two

Write the missing letters to complete the words.

said

s	a	i	d
s	a	i	d
s	a	i	d
s	a	i	d

with

w		t	h
w	i	t	
w			h

again

a		a		n
	g	a		
			i	n

laugh

l					h
			a	u	
					g

Unjumble the letters and write the words on the lines.

aanig	dasi	twhi	ghula
____	____	____	____

Learning Goal: Review the high-frequency words said, with, again, and laugh.

Write the missing letters to complete the words.

what

w			t
			t
		a	t

some

s			e
		m	e
s		m	e

which

w	h			h
		i	c	h
w				h

asked

a			e	d
			e	d
		s	k	

Unjumble the letters and write the words on the lines.

hatw	meos	kaeds	ichwh
____	____	____	____

Learning Goal: Review the high-frequency words what, some, which, and asked.

When two consonants are together in a word it is called a consonant blend. Colour the words that begin with r consonant blends.

grapes

fox

mitten

tree

grass

sled

plane

wolf

frog

crab

tent

maple leaf

Learning Goal: Learn about r consonant blends at the beginning of words.

16

ACROSS

2. Susie is an artist. She likes to

___ ___ ___ ___.

4. A giant ___ ___ ___ ___ ___ ___

lived in the castle and blew fire at

visitors.

5. The green ___ ___ ___ ___

hopped into the water.

DOWN

1. The queen wore a

___ ___ ___ ___ ___.

3. What should I

___ ___ ___ ___ ___ to the party?

Learning Goal: Learn about r consonant blends at the beginning of words.

BL

CL

FL

SL

PL

Learning Goal: Learn about l consonant blends at the beginning of words.

Find the words that begin with l consonant blends in the word search below.

R A P Z N N C S I Z
X V M L V P W D U R
G A L F A M Y C E S
M S Z Z S T A E R T
L U K R W O E Q P C
M O E C B W L U W Y
Y V N K O O C P N B
D N C L A L E D M V
Z M G R O V B S W S
H O E U L B Q F L E
J S D B D O Q T O O
D T R L V H A R Q I

BLOCKS   GLOW   FLAG
BLUE   PLATE   CLOUD

Learning Goal: Learn about l consonant blends at the beginning of words.

19

Fill in the missing letters to complete the words that begin with s consonant blends.

_ _ _ ake

_ _ _ ar

_ _ _ ovel

_ _ _ ell

_ _ _ eat

_ _ _ ark

_ _ _ oon

_ _ _ im

_ _ _ eep

Colour the stars with words that begin with s consonant blends.

star same snake

snail sour school

soup surf spoon

square slide small

Learning Goal: Learn about s consonant blends at the beginning of words.

21

Review consonant blends by filling in each column with the missing words from the word bank.

swim   clam   star   play   cloud   sweat

L BLEND

_ _ a _

_ l _ y

_ _ _ _ d

S BLEND

_ _ i _

_ _ _ _ t

_ _ _ r

Learning Goal: Review l, s, and r consonant blends at the beginning of words.

Review consonant blends by filling in each column with the missing words from the word bank.

cat   game   crab   frog   dragon   ram

R BLEND

_ r _ _

_ _ a _ _

d _ _ _ _ _ _

NO BLENDS

_ a _ _

_ _ _ e _

_ _ t _

Learning Goal: Review l, s, and r consonant blends at the beginning of words.

23

Vowels can make both long and short sounds. Short a sounds like the a in <u>cat</u>. Colour the things in the picture that make the short a sound.

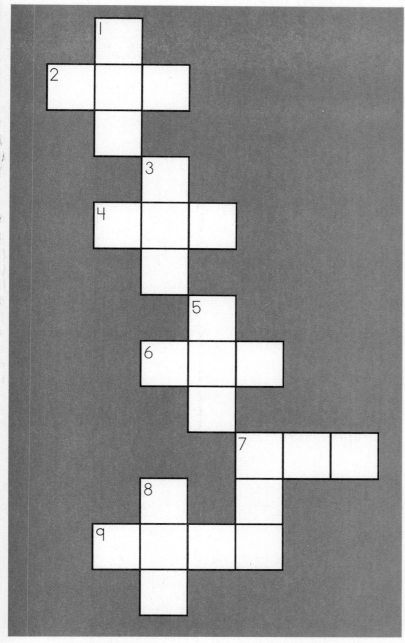

ACROSS

2. Something you wear on your head.

4. Something you put on a sandwich.

6. Something you cook in.

7. Something soda comes in.

9. Something found on a boat.

DOWN

1. Something you carry things in.

3. Something found at your front door.

5. Something you hit a baseball with.

7. A pet that says meow.

8. A sports follower.

Learning Goal: Learn about short a vowel sounds.

Long a sounds like the a in <u>cake</u>. Complete the sentences by using words that make the long a sound from the word bank.

game	gate	May	tape	make
	same	plate	late	cake

1. Today is the big ___ ___ ___ ___.

2. Open the ___ ___ ___ ___ to let the dog out.

3. My sister and I have the ___ ___ ___ ___ shirt.

4. There are three cookies on the ___ ___ ___ ___ ___.

5. I need ___ ___ ___ ___ for my project.

6. My birthday is in ___ ___ ___.

7. We will need eggs to make a ___ ___ ___ ___.

8. I like to ___ ___ ___ ___ cookies.

9. I'm going to be ___ ___ ___ ___ for the party.

Learning Goal: Learn about long a vowel sounds.

Follow the maze to help Charlie find the party so he can eat some cake.

Learning Goal: Learn about long a vowel sounds.

Short e sounds like the e in <u>vet</u>. Colour the picture of the words that make the short e sound.

egg

dog

top

hat

hen

van

elephant

jam

net

tree

vet

elf

```
J E B C E G D D N I
P M F J G D S E P C
E Y V E N T H D Y I
T T G E M S B J O N
E R O K A E O Q L J
N I Z X E V Y N Q F
W L K C W N X R K P
T L B C R X V D I O
Z E B K G Z K C X F
W P L Z S S Q K T Z
H S J C T E L Y O H
I F W E N T G E L Z
```

WEB	SET	LEG	TEN	WENT
HEN	END	EGG	SPELL	VEST

Learning Goal: Learn about short e vowel sounds.

29

Long e sounds like the e in <u>leaf</u>. Words with ee and ea make the long e sound.
Draw a line to match the picture to the correct word that makes the long e sound.

eel

leaf

beach

eagle

bee

green

wheel

Learning Goal: Learn about long e vowel sounds.

Use the clues to fill in the blanks below with words that make the long e sound from the word bank.

| eel | beach | green | eagle |
| wheel | leaf | bee |

1. I fly in the sky.

   I am an ___ ___ ___ ___ ___.

2. I am a great place to visit on a hot day.

   I am the ___ ___ ___ ___ ___.

3. I am electric!

   I am an ___ ___ ___.

4. I am an emblem of Canada.

   I am a maple ___ ___ ___ ___.

5. I help your bike move.

   I am a ___ ___ ___ ___ ___.

6. I have black and yellow stripes on my body.

   I am a ___ ___ ___.

7. I am the color of the forest.

   I am ___ ___ ___ ___ ___.

Learning Goal: Learn about long e vowel sounds.

Short i sounds like the i in <u>crib</u>. Colour the pictures of words that make the short i sound.

wig

pig

box

net

moose

ten

deer

bib

lip

puffin

hat

jersey

Learning Goal: Learn about short i vowel sounds.

Use the clues to solve the crossword puzzle with words that make the short i sound.

ACROSS

1. Something you do when you drink.

3. The largest organ on your body.

6. Something found on a fish.

7. Dogs do this to look for bones.

9. Another name for he.

10. When you come in first place.

DOWN

2. Something you wear on your shirt.

4. Another name for child or baby goat.

5. Something you did when you played hide-and-seek.

8. Something you teach your dog.

Learning Goal: Learn about short i vowel sounds.

Long i sounds like the i in <u>kite</u>. Complete the sentences below by using the words that make the long i sound from the word bank.

nine	lime	fine	dime	slide
	bike	kite	line	hide

1. I have ___ ___ ___ ___ balloons.

2. A ___ ___ ___ ___ is green and very sour.

3. I am ___ ___ ___ ___. How are you?

4. My dog loves to ___ ___ ___ ___.

5. I love to go fast down the ___ ___ ___ ___ ___.

6. My ___ ___ ___ ___ is very colourful.

7. I waited in ___ ___ ___ ___ for five minutes.

8. Can I borrow a ___ ___ ___ ___?

9. I ride my ___ ___ ___ ___ to school.

Learning Goal: Learn about long i vowel sounds.

Follow the maze to help Mike find his kite.

Learning Goal: Learn about long i vowel sounds.

Short o sounds like the o in <u>box</u>. Draw a line to match the picture to the correct word that makes the short o sound.

fox

dog

pot

jog

rob

rod

mop

Learning Goal: Learn about short o vowel sounds.

Use the word bank to find the words with a short o sound in the word search.

```
I  W  N  L  B  Z  W  Q  O  K
X  A  R  O  C  K  D  Q  X  S
D  Z  S  L  E  K  G  R  E  I
O  S  O  T  P  O  P  S  I  I
R  D  G  O  D  S  V  G  C  I
N  X  Q  O  A  B  S  B  X  N
V  E  Z  G  R  T  O  H  E  T
Y  F  F  W  N  F  C  S  O  R
G  E  I  V  H  U  K  D  Q  K
D  I  L  H  Z  K  T  T  K  Y
T  E  O  K  Z  I  B  A  W  E
N  N  O  G  A  G  Z  W  M  S
```

| DOG | FROG | ROD | ROCK | DOT |
| SOB | BOSS | HOT | SOCK | POP |

Learning Goal: Learn about short o vowel sounds.

Long o sounds like the o in <u>bone</u>. Complete the sentences by using the words that make the long o sound from the word bank.

ghost	snow	note	no	rope
pillow	phone	loan	road	

1. I saw a ___ ___ ___ ___ ___ on Halloween.

2. The ___ ___ ___ ___ ___ rang three times.

3. When I sleep I always use a ___ ___ ___ ___ ___ ___.

4. Climb the ___ ___ ___ ___ to get to the treehouse.

5. I wrote you a ___ ___ ___ ___.

6. I play in the ___ ___ ___ ___.

7. ___ ___, you may not borrow my ice skates.

8. I will ___ ___ ___ ___ you my hat.

9. That ___ ___ ___ ___ leads to the school.

 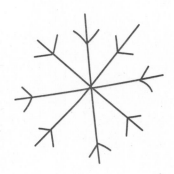 

Learning Goal: Learn about long o vowel sounds.

bone	ghost	goat	snow
	rose	coat	soap

1. Dogs love me.

    I am a ___ ___ ___ ___.

2. I say "Boo!"

    I am a ___ ___ ___ ___ ___.

3. You wear me when you are cold.

    I am a ___ ___ ___ ___.

4. You use me when you take a bath.

    I am ___ ___ ___ ___.

5. I have horns.

    I am a ___ ___ ___ ___.

6. You see me in the winter.

    I am ___ ___ ___ ___.

7. I am a type of flower.

    I am a ___ ___ ___ ___.

Learning Goal: Learn about long o vowel sounds.

Short u sounds like u in <u>bus</u>. Colour the pictures of words that make the short u sound.

sun

syrup

can

fire

nut

pup

bus

hut

lobster

mug

leaf

log

Learning Goal: Learn about short u vowel sounds.

Use the clues to solve the crossword puzzle with words that make the short u sound.

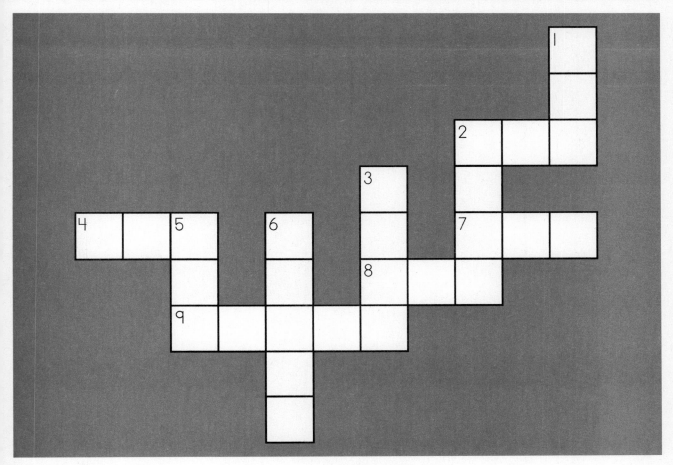

ACROSS

2. You keep water in this.

4. What you see on a nice day.

7. You can drink hot beverages out of this.

8. You can drink cold beverages out of this.

9. This is a vehicle with a bed.

DOWN

1. Something you do when something is stuck.

2. Something you do when playing with a skipping rope.

3. An animal that floats on water.

5. Something a squirrel loves.

6. Your shortest finger.

Learning Goal: Learn about short u vowel sounds.

Long u sounds like the u in <u>blue</u>. Complete the sentences by using the words that make the long u sound from the word bank.

mule	use	cube	glue	tune
tube	blue	juice	cute	

1. I need ___ ___ ___ ___ for my project.

2. My favourite colour is ___ ___ ___ ___.

3. That kitten is so ___ ___ ___ ___.

4. What is your favourite kind of ___ ___ ___ ___ ___.

5. You have to ___ ___ ___ ___ musical instruments.

6. A ___ ___ ___ ___ lives on the farm.

7. Ice comes out in the shape of a ___ ___ ___ ___.

8. Toothpaste comes in a ___ ___ ___ ___.

9. I ___ ___ ___ a pencil when I am writing.

Follow the maze to help Emily find her juice.

Learning Goal: Learn about long u vowel sounds.

A noun can be a person, place, animal, or thing. Colour the nouns below using the key.

If the noun is a person, colour it red.
If the noun is a place, colour it green.

If the noun is an animal, colour it orange.
If the noun is a thing, colour it blue.

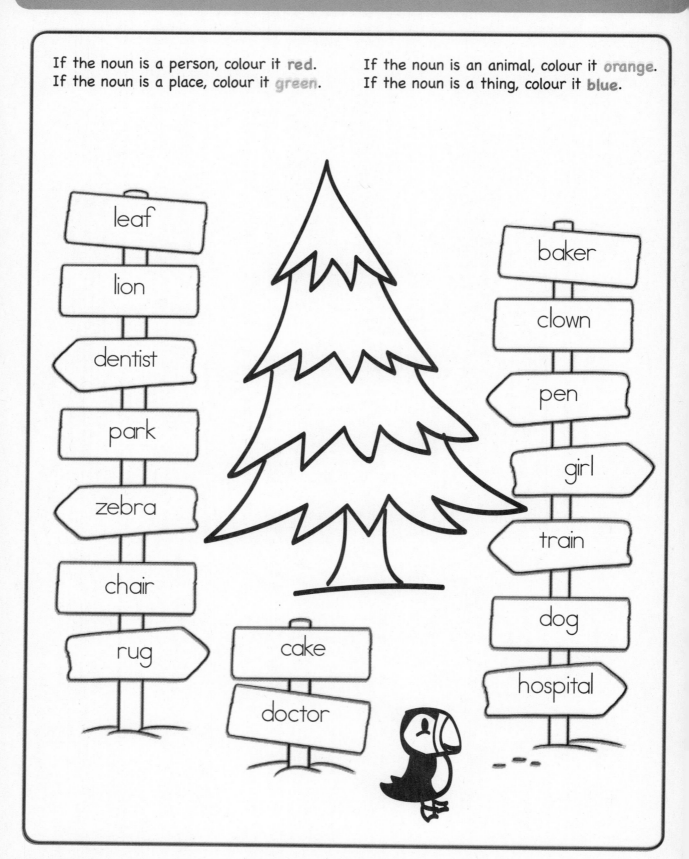

leaf

lion

dentist

park

zebra

chair

rug

cake

doctor

baker

clown

pen

girl

train

dog

hospital

Learning Goal: Develop an awareness of nouns. Identify, write, and use nouns appropriately.

44

Write each noun from the word bank in the correct category.

nurse beach ruler tiger library kitchen bear
shoe butcher school hat farmer church brother
crocodile pilot bicycle teacher Toronto computer
fox giraffe van cow

Person

1. _____
2. _____
3. _____
4. _____
5. _____
6. _____

Place

1. _____
2. _____
3. _____
4. _____
5. _____
6. _____

Animal

1. _____
2. _____
3. _____
4. _____
5. _____
6. _____

Thing

1. _____
2. _____
3. _____
4. _____
5. _____
6. _____

Learning Goal: Develop an awareness of nouns. Identify, write, and use nouns appropriately.

Find all of the nouns below and write them on the closet doors.

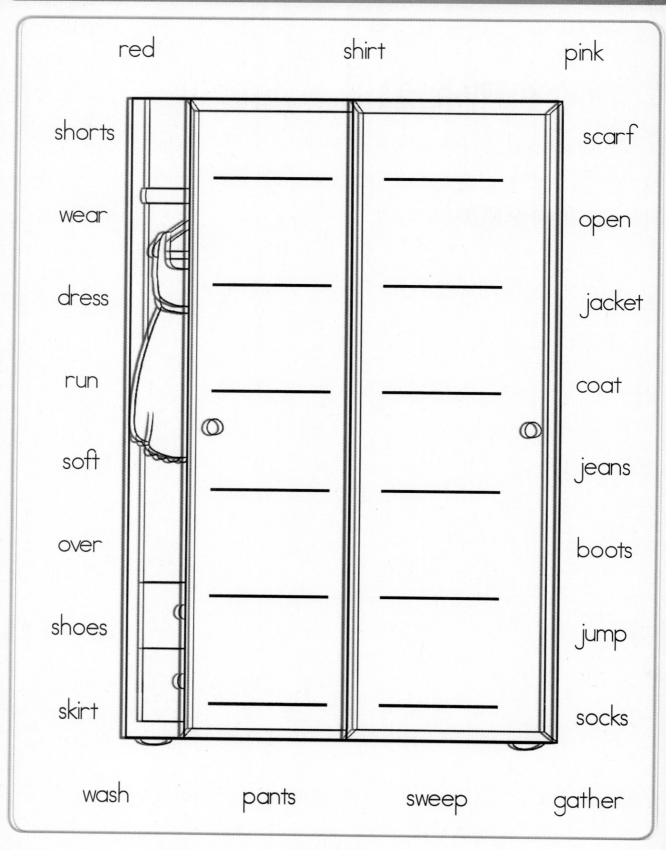

red   shirt   pink

shorts   scarf

wear   open

dress   jacket

run   coat

soft   jeans

over   boots

shoes   jump

skirt   socks

wash   pants   sweep   gather

Learning Goal: Develop an awareness of nouns. Identify, write, and use nouns appropriately.

46

Solve each puzzle using a noun from the word bank.

| June | calf | kettle | Tuesday | summer | tractor |

1. The season after spring:

2. You boil water in this:

3. The month after May:

4. A farmer drives this:

5. The day after Monday:

6. A young cow:

Learning Goal: Develop an awareness of nouns. Identify, write, and use nouns appropriately.

Follow the directions below to write plural nouns.

When making some words plural we add an s.

Example: one bird 🐤   two birds 🐤🐤

1. cup _____   6. team _____

2. boat _____   7. kitten _____

3. boy _____   8. computer _____

4. horse _____   9. phone _____

5. rabbit _____   10. paper _____

When making some words plural we add an es. Words ending in sh, ch, ss, s and x need es to make more than one.

Example: a peach 🍎   some peaches 🍎🍎🍎

1. glass _____   6. watch _____

2. witch _____   7. kiss _____

3. dress _____   8. match _____

4. fox _____   9. dish _____

5. bush _____   10. box _____

Learning Goal: Develop an awareness of plurals and the ability to change words from the singular to the plural.

Follow the directions below to write plural nouns.

Some plurals change y to i, and add es.

Example: a cherry   lots of cherries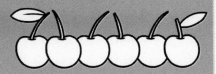

1. puppy _____

2. berry _____

3. copy _____

4. fly _____

5. army _____

6. bully _____

7. pony _____

8. daisy _____

9. lady _____

10. party _____

11. family _____

12. ruby _____

13. story _____

14. enemy _____

15. city _____

16. bunny _____

17. kitty _____

18. baby _____

19. buddy _____

20. body _____

Learning Goal: Develop an awareness of plurals and the ability to change words from the singular to the plural.

Verbs are doing or action words. Read the words on the fish below and colour the fish with verbs. The first one is done for you.

Choose the correct verb for each sentence.

1. Fish _____ water weeds. (swim, eat, look)

2. Fish _____ through gills in the water.

(walk, bang, breathe)

3. Fish _____ fins to help them to swim. (have, has, was)

4. Ken _____ a large brown trout. (catch, caught, called)

Learning Goal: Develop an awareness of verbs. Identify, write, and use verbs appropriately.

Write the verbs on the stones to get to the treasure.

pencil

cake

eat

run

jump

dance

city

small

drink

school

banana

finger

goat

speak

yellow

boat

candy

read

skip

kick

pie

Start

Learning Goal: Develop an awareness of verbs. Identify, write, and use verbs appropriately.

skate

rink

fish

rod

climb

rock

sleep

tent

play

ball

build

man

ski

snow

water

swim

Learning Goal: Develop an awareness of verbs. Identify, write, and use verbs appropriately.

Adjectives are descriptive words that describe a person, place, or thing. Circle the adjectives in each sentence.

Example: cute and red.
The cute kitten played with a ball of red wool.

1. The dog dug a deep hole in the garden.

2. Grandma baked a delicious cake for my birthday.

3. Tara wears pink bows in her hair.

4. Dan likes fluffy marshmallows in his hot chocolate.

5. Ben rode his skateboard down the steep hill.

6. Black and white badgers live in the woodlands.

7. Early morning is the time to hear birds sing.

8. The grumpy giant knocked down the tall trees.

9 The sleepy kitten took a nap.

10. The tall buildings glistened in the bright sun.

11. The smart camper knew what to do.

12. The ice skater was so beautiful.

13. The red and white flag was waving in the wind.

14. The small black bear cub walked into the woods.

15. The slippery fish swam away.

Learning Goal: Develop an awareness of adjectives. Identify, write, and use adjectives appropriately.

Circle the adjective with a similar meaning as the word in red. The first one is done for you.

small	loud	unhappy	mean
big	soft	sad	kind
(little)	mean	angry	clever
tall	noisy	joyful	cruel

smart	different	great	enormous
happy	bright	wise	small
wise	silly	wonderful	slippy
old	strange	fine	large

sour	huge	funny	tasty
bitter	tiny	friendly	delicious
sweet	gigantic	silly	shallow
salty	hollow	scary	cool

Write the adjectives from the hats above in the sentences below.

1. A whale is an _____ sea creature.

2. A lemon has a _____ taste.

3. The _____ music hurt my ears.

4. Owls are thought to be _____ birds.

5. It would be _____ if everyone could be friends.

6. Jenny cried because she was _____ .

7. Dad ate _____ pasta at the restaurant.

8. A _____ ant can carry a large twig.

9. Keith dressed as a _____ wizard for Halloween.

10 Mom's hair is a _____ colour from mine.

Learning Goal: Develop an awareness of adjectives. Identify, write, and use adjectives appropriately.

54

Follow the directions below to colour the animals.

Colour the **longer** snake **blue**.
Colour the **shorter** caterpillar red and **brown**.
Colour the **taller** giraffe orange.
Colour the **bigger** frog green.
Colour the **smaller** snail yellow.

Learning Goal: Develop an awareness of adjectives. Identify, write, and use adjectives appropriately.

55

Write two adjectives to describe each picture.

Learning Goal: Develop an awareness of adjectives. Identify, write, and use adjectives appropriately.

Write each word from the word bank in the correct category.

fox run soft cold beaver sleep eat
book happy smart skis green polar bear
maple syrup jump small laugh learn

NOUN	VERB	ADJECTIVE
_____	_____	_____
_____	_____	_____
_____	_____	_____
_____	_____	_____
_____	_____	_____

Learning Goal: Identify, write, and use verbs, nouns, and adjectives appropriately.

Josh   Puddles   skate   cuddly   treats   parks
polar bears   eat   long   Canada   green   pretty

1. _____ loves to play with his _____ puppy.
   noun   adjective

2. Sara likes to _____ _____ grapes.
                  verb   adjective

3. My dog _____ loves _____.
          noun   noun

4. My hair is _____.
              adjective

5. Look at the _____ sunset.
               adjective

6. I love to _____.
             verb

7. _____ _____ are my favourite animal.
   noun

8. I love _____ because of the beautiful _____.
          noun   noun

Learning Goal: Identify, write, and use verbs, nouns, and adjectives appropriately.

Synonyms are words with similar meanings. Match the synonyms to the pictures. The first one is done for you.

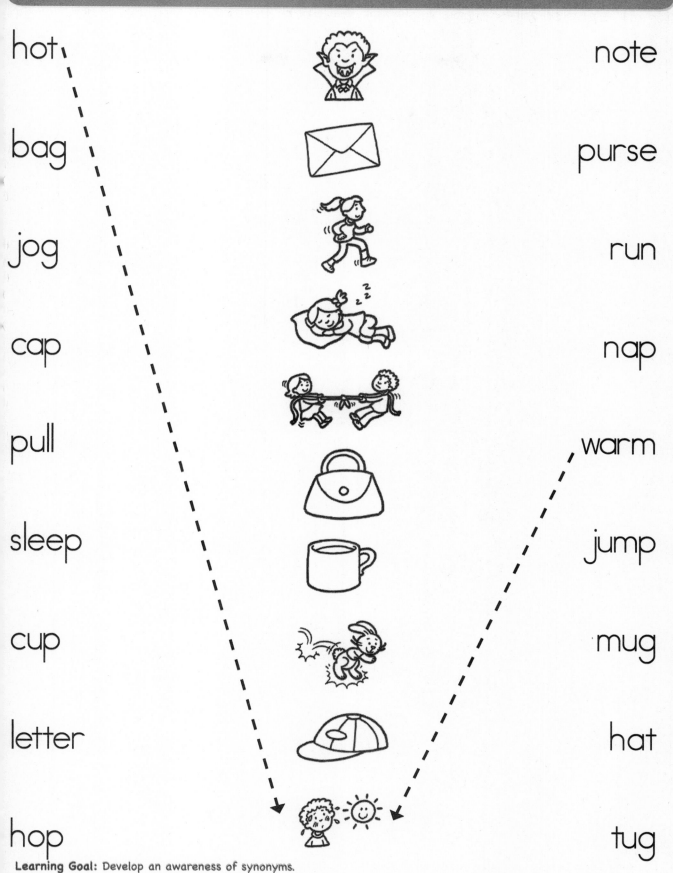

hot

bag

jog

cap

pull

sleep

cup

letter

hop

note

purse

run

nap

warm

jump

mug

hat

tug

Learning Goal: Develop an awareness of synonyms.

fast	quick	slow	walk
yell	talk	quiet	shout
small	huge	bear	little
pretty	scary	beautiful	tiny
wet	damp	dry	drip
happy	mad	sad	glad
right	wrong	correct	left

Learning Goal: Develop an awareness of synonyms.

Antonyms are two words that have opposite meanings. Look at the pictures and write the antonyms on the lines. The first one is done for you.

awake

asleep

Learning Goal: Develop an awareness of antonyms.

Draw a line to match the antonyms. The first one is done for you.

quick	dark
walk	happy
light	found
good	slow
sad	bottom
lost	out
top	up
under	run
in	over
off	on
down	bad

Learning Goal: Develop an awareness of antonyms.

Write the antonym of each word and draw a picture in the yellow box of the word you wrote. The first one is done for you.

up   down   open   _____

cold   _____   white   _____

happy   _____   girl   _____

day   _____   go   _____

Learning Goal: Develop an awareness of antonyms.

63

Learning Goal: Correctly identify synonyms using pictures.

Learning Goal: Correctly identify antonyms using pictures.

Homonyms are words that sound alike but have different meanings and spellings. Read the words below and circle the correct honomym for each word.

sun	son	sew	set
bear	base	bare	barn
deer	dare	deep	dear
hole	hour	hand	whole
no	now	knew	know
won	own	one	run
eye	I	ear	eat

Learning Goal: Develop an awareness of homonyms.

Write the correct to, two, or too in each sentence.

To: Mom likes to dance. Dad went to the park.

Two: I have two arms.

Too: I like popcorn too.

to
two
too

1. A cat has _____ eyes and _____ ears.

2. Tom is eight years old and Pat is eight, _____.

3. Sam is going _____ the bowling alley.

4. Koalas like _____ eat leaves.

5. It is _____ cold for many animals to live in Antarctica.

6. Nessa tries _____ jump on the bed sometimes.

7. I want to play hockey, _____.

8. There are _____ birds on the fence.

9. I went _____ the park, _____.

10. Polar bears walk _____ the ice from their dens.

11. There are _____ puffins on the rock.

12. I want to go sledding. Do you want _____ come, _____?

Learning Goal: Recognize, write, and use to, two, and too accurately.

Use the first letter of each picture to make a new word. Write the letters on the lines. The first one is done for you.

bear + antlers + tent = b a t

pie + eagle + 10 = _ _ _

puffin + plank + net = _ _ _

zebra + ice skates + polar bear = _ _ _

pig + lion + ant + snail = _ _ _ _

log + apple + mountain + panda = _ _ _ _

Learning Goal: Create new words by using letters from common first words.

Create compound words by combining common first words. Use the word bank and pictures to fill in the blanks. The first one is done for you.

butter	house	hand	light	fly	bag	arm	sun
foot	chair	ball	star	boy	fish	cow	flower

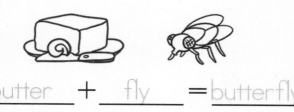

butter ___ + ___ fly ___ = butterfly

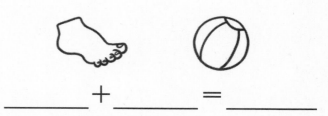

___ + ___ = ___

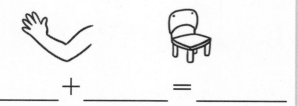

___ + ___ = ___

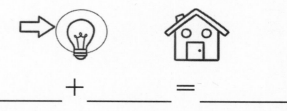

___ + ___ = ___

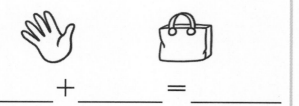

___ + ___ = ___

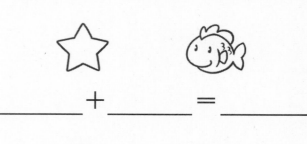

___ + ___ = ___

___ + ___ = ___

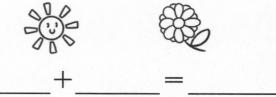

___ + ___ = ___

Write the two words in each of these words. The first one is done for you.

1. classroom = _class_ + _room_

2. birthday = ___ + ___

3. snowman = ___ + ___

4. somewhere = ___ + ___

5. seaside = ___ + ___

6. goldfish = ___ + ___

7. blackbird = ___ + ___

8. hedgehog = ___ + ___

Learning Goal: Create compound words by combining common first words.

Follow the maze to connect the pictures to make a new word.

What new word did you make?

_____

Learning Goal: Identify and successfully combine different words to form a compound word.

Write the missing words to complete the sentences below. Use the words from the word bank.

over	Once	them	who	children
make	many	about	were	said

1. The _____ played with the toys.

2. Tom kicked the ball _____ the wall.

3. "Time for bed," _____ Mom.

4. There _____ lots of children in the park.

5. Do you know _____ that puck belongs to?

6. There are _____ twelve cookies in the jar.

7. Do you know any of _____?

8. _____ upon a time...

9. What should we _____ in art class?

10. There are so _____ puffins in the park.

Learning Goal: Recognize, write, and use high-frequency words accurately.

Colour a box for each word that fits in each column. The first one is done for you.

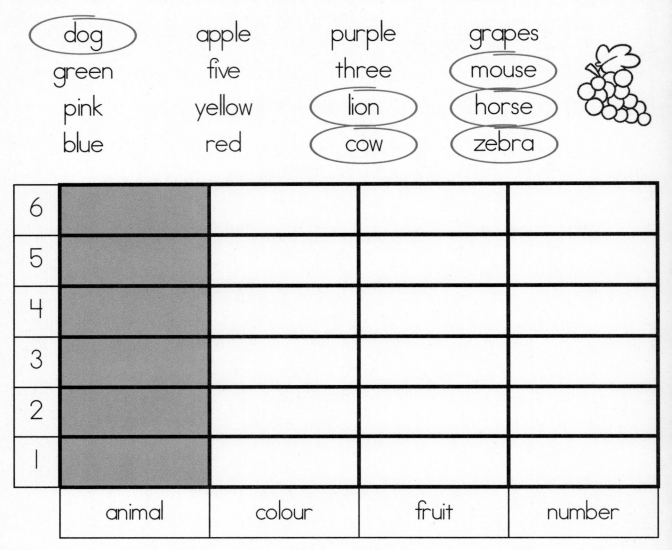

dog apple purple grapes
green five three mouse
pink yellow lion horse
blue red cow zebra

	animal	colour	fruit	number
6				
5				
4				
3				
2				
1				

Complete the sentences below.

1. My favourite fruit is _____.

2. My favourite number is _____.

3. My favourite colour is _____.

4. My favourite animal is a _____.

Learning Goal: Read, write, and colour accordingly.

Write the missing words to complete the sentences below. Use the words from the word bank.

girl	happy	little	write	Would
house	school	other	How	store

1. The _____ opened at nine o'clock.

2. Zara was _____ with her new puppy.

3. I will _____ a story.

4. I go to _____ every day.

5. My _____ has a door, windows, and a roof.

6. My _____ sister is younger than me.

7. The _____ flavor of ice cream is my favourite.

8. _____ many people will be at the party?

9. _____ you like to go ice skating?

10. The _____ who rides the bus is in my class.

Learning Goal: Recognize, write, and use high-frequency words accurately.

1. baker   tractor

2. pilot   oven

3. gardener   shovel

4. nurse   airplane

5. jockey   horse

6. farmer   needle

Write yes or no to answer each question.

1. Does a doctor bake bread?   _____ .

2. Does a baker cut hair?   _____ .

3. Does a vet look after animals?   _____ .

4. Does a dentist grow crops?   _____ .

5. Does a butcher sell meat?   _____ .

6. Does a jockey ride a dog?   _____ .

Draw a picture of something that these people use at work.	
artist	farmer

Learning Goal: Read, match, write, and draw accordingly.

74

Draw a line to match the animal to the baby animal. The first one is done for you.

cow   lamb

dog   kitten

sheep   calf

cat   puppy

horse   duckling

duck   foal

Use the word bank to write the correct word to complete each sentence.

cub	kid	piglet	gosling
tadpole	chick	spiderling	

1. A young goat is a _____.

2. A young goose is a _____.

3. A young lion is a _____.

4. A young pig is a _____.

5. A young frog is a _____.

6. A young spider is a _____.

7. A young bird is a _____.

Learning Goal: Read, match, write, and draw accordingly.

Read each clue below and colour the correct balloon. Then write the word on the line.

1. I am a four-letter word with ee in the middle. _____

2. I am the only three-letter word. _____

3. Put the letter t in front of the word here. _____

4. I am the opposite of right. _____

5. I am the only question word. _____

6. I am a five-letter word with three vowels. _____

7. Change the letter m in maid to the letter s. _____

8. I am another word for small. _____

9. I am the opposite of under. _____

B. The leftover word.

1. What word is left over? _____

2. Write a clue for it. _____

Learning Goal: Recognize and write the high-frequency words. Solve word clues.

balloon	asked	before	once	being	their

already	caught	below	course	birthday	than

1. I have the word for inside me. _____

2. 🎭 – m + ed = _____

3. I am the only eight-letter word. _____

4. I rhyme with ran. _____

5. Fairytales start with this word. _____

6. ⚾ + oo + n = _____

7. I have the letter t at the end. _____

8. 🐝 – e + low = _____

9. I have the letter y at the end. _____

10. I have the word our in the middle. _____

11. rieht is how you spell me backwards. _____

12. I am an ing word with less than six letters. _____

Unjumble the words and write them below.

1. ekdas = _____   4. areadly = _____

2. foerbe = _____   5. thbriday = _____

3. ocne = _____   6. htier = _____

Learning Goal: Recognize and write high-frequency words accurately. Solve word clues.

Remember to use a capital letter:
- at the start of the sentence
- for names of people and places
- for I
- for days, months, and special days

tuesday	pencil	france	mary	july
england	bicycle	piano	wednesday	house
football	ben	scooter	december	christmas

Write these sentences using the correct capital letters.

1. megan plays soccer with her friend kate.

_____

2. i would like to go to vancouver in july.

_____

3. joe and ella dress up for halloween.

_____

4. i eat a chocolate egg on easter sunday.

_____

Name each pet. Remember to use a capital letter.

_____ _____ _____ _____

Learning Goal: Review how to use capital letters appropriately.

A sentence always starts with a capital letter and ends with a period.
Write these sentences with a capital letter and period.

1. the lady bought milk

   _____

2. my teacher is friendly

   _____

3. june is my favourite month

   _____

4. the sun is yellow and bright

   _____

5. i love watching hockey

   _____

6. amy and grace are coming over

   _____

7. today is the last day of school

   _____

Learning Goal: Review how to use correct punctuation and capitalization.

1. The girl is singing a song.
   The boy likes skipping.

_____

2. The dogs are barking loudly.
   Dad is making a cake.

_____

3. Koalas can climb trees.
   A boy is walking his dog.

_____

4. A train moves on tracks.
   Sam is reading his book.

_____

5. The girls are on the bus.
   The farmer is milking the cow.

_____

Learning Goal: Develop awareness of correct sentence structure.

Write the words below in the correct order to complete the sentences.

1. is   penguin   A   bird.   a

_____

2. extinct.   are   Dinosaurs

_____

3. An   has   a   elephant   trunk.   long

_____

4. lions   called   Baby   cubs.   are

_____

Write each word in its correct place.

1. A _____ lives in a _____. (dog, kennel)

2. A _____ lives in a _____. (nest, bird)

3. A _____ lives in the _____. (sea, fish)

4. A _____ lives in a _____. (horse, stable)

5. A _____ lives in a _____. (web, spider)

Learning Goal: Develop awareness of correct sentence structure.

1. likes to Dan eat oranges.

_____

2. Kate a red has strawberry.

_____

3. ate The an hedgehog apple.

_____

4. are grapes Bananas fruit. and

_____

Write each word in its correct place.

1. A _____ is a _____. (grape, fruit)

2. An _____ is a _____. (vegetable, onion)

3. A _____ is a _____. (banana, fruit)

4. A _____ is a _____. (fruit, kiwi)

5. A _____ is a _____. (vegetable, turnip)

Learning Goal: Develop awareness of correct sentence structure.

It is raining.
Evan can write.
went to   Bob is sad.
Jeff wants to   I am in school.
Ben is a boy.   at the shop
all off   told us   Mum and Des
clean and   with my   A witch
A cat purrs.   sat on   It's my birthday.
Jan eats fruit.   You run to   Dogs chew bones.
Bees make honey.   by the door   The fire is hot.
see the   Doctors can   in the pram   The library was open.
under me   Pigs can   Some dinosaurs ate plants.
Dragons are   Fred bought a mobile phone.   Minecraft is
The team will   climbing mountains   reading is
Some rivers flow down mountains.

Write four of the sentences you circled on the lines below.

1. _____

2. _____

3. _____

4. _____

Learning Goal: Develop an awareness of sentence structure. Write sentences accurately.

Build a sentence from the cauldron. Then write it on the lines below. The first one is done for you.

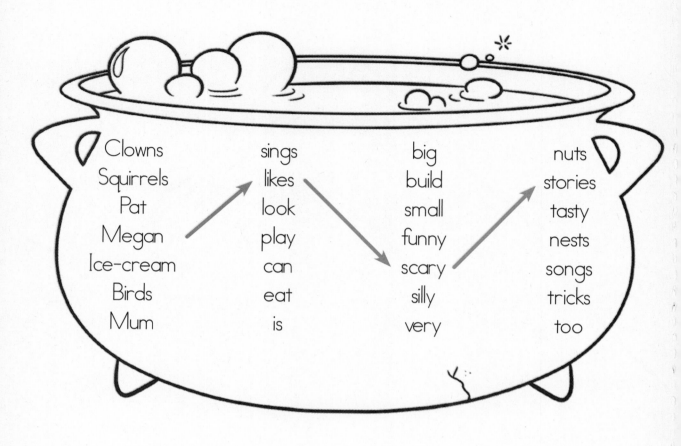

Clowns	sings	big	nuts
Squirrels	likes	build	stories
Pat	look	small	tasty
Megan	play	funny	nests
Ice-cream	can	scary	songs
Birds	eat	silly	tricks
Mum	is	very	too

1. Megan likes scary stories.

2. Clowns

3. Squirrels

4.

5.

6.

7.

Learning Goal: Develop an awareness of sentence structure. Write sentences correctly.

Write your own sentences about the picture below.

1. _____ .

2. _____ .

3. _____ .

4. _____ .

5. _____ .

6. _____ .

7. _____ .

8. _____ .

Learning Goal: Develop an awareness of sentence structure. Write sentences correctly.

| John | Anna | Zara | Alex | Tom |

1. How many people are at the bus stop? _____

2. Who is first? _____

3. Who is last? _____

4. Where in the line is Anna? _____

Read the sentences and colour the picture.

Tom has brown hair and is wearing a green sweater and blue jeans. Zara is wearing a beautiful red dress. John's brown hair is the same colour as his sweater. Anna is wearing a yellow skirt and top. She has a pink coat. She always wears ribbons in her hair to match her skirt and top.

Learning Goal: Read, write, and colour accordingly.

Read the sentences below. Draw the missing elements to complete the picture.

1. Draw a fish at the end of the fishing rod.
2. Draw a bird in the sky.
3. Draw a hat on Dad's head.
4. Draw two fish in the water.
5. Draw the sun in the sky.

Read the sentences and colour the picture.

Max and his dad are fishing in their old, grey boat.
The blue water is clear. Max feels warm in his green T-shirt.
Dad's red hat is keeping the bright yellow sun out of his
eyes. They wish they had worn shorts instead of blue jeans,
because it is so hot.

Learning Goal: Read, write, and colour accordingly.

1. Draw a smaller tree beside the tree.
2. Draw a nest in the bigger tree.
3. Draw a bird in the nest.
4. Draw a kite over the smaller tree.
5. Draw a cloud above the kite.
6. Draw a rabbit under the bigger tree.
7. Draw a snail below the smaller tree.
8. Draw some flowers in the grass between the trees.
9. Draw a butterfly by the flowers.

Check the boxes next to the sentences that are true.

1. The bird is in the smaller tree. ☐

2. The kite is under the cloud. ☐

3. The rabbit is in the smaller tree. ☐

4. The cloud is under the rabbit. ☐

Learning Goal: Read, write, and draw accordingly.

I have eight legs.
I spin a web.

I am a _____.

You drink me.
I come from cows.

I am _____.

I can swim.
I have gills.

I am a _____.

I live on a farm.
I have wool as my coat.

I am a _____.

I am yellow.
You can eat me.
I am a fruit.

I am a _____.

I am a zoo animal.
I look like a horse.
I am black and white.

I am a _____.

Learning Goal: Read, respond, and draw accordingly..

Read the clues below. Then write the name of each child in the ovals below their picture.

1. Matt is wearing a yellow shirt. Matt likes to read.

2. Tara plays with her brown teddy bear.

3. Joe plays soccer after school.

4. Beth is wearing winter clothes.

5. Evan has a pet dog.

6. Abby has black hair and loves flowers.

Answer the questions using the pictures above.

1. Who has red hair? _____

2. Who has flowers? _____

3. Which boy has black hair? _____

Learning Goal: Read, write, and match accordingly.

1. Colour the top window brown.
2. Colour the window beside the door blue.
3. Draw two flower boxes beneath the other downstairs windows.
4. Draw more shingles on the roof.
5. Draw four red flowers to the left of the house.
6. Draw a yellow sun above the house.
7. Draw some clouds underneath the sun.
8. Draw a green bush to the right of the house.
9. Draw a blackbird sitting on the roof.

Learning Goal: Read, colour, and draw accordingly.

Read the clues below. Then colour the correct picture.

1 I live in your garden.
I slide along the ground.
I have a shell.

2 I am brown and hard.
I grow on a tree.
Squirrels eat me.

3 I come out at night.
I can fly.
I sleep upside-down.

4 I have four wheels.
I work on a farm.
I carry heavy loads.

5 I keep you warm.
I am soft.
You wear me on your head.

6 I have four legs.
I have a mane.
I hunt for my dinner.

Learning Goal: Read and colour accordingly.

Read the sentences below. Draw and colour the missing elements to complete the picture.

1. Colour the chair blue and yellow.
2. Draw a flag on top of the sandcastle.
3. Colour the larger beach ball red and green.
4. Draw a seagull flying between the umbrella and the palm tree.
5. How many crabs do you see? Write the number on a cloud.
6. Write the number of seashells on the island.
7. Colour each section of the umbrella a different colour.
8. Draw a sun to the right of the island.
9. Colour two shells pink, and three shells brown.

Learning Goal: Read, colour, and draw accordingly.

Write the letters below each number to discover the secret words.

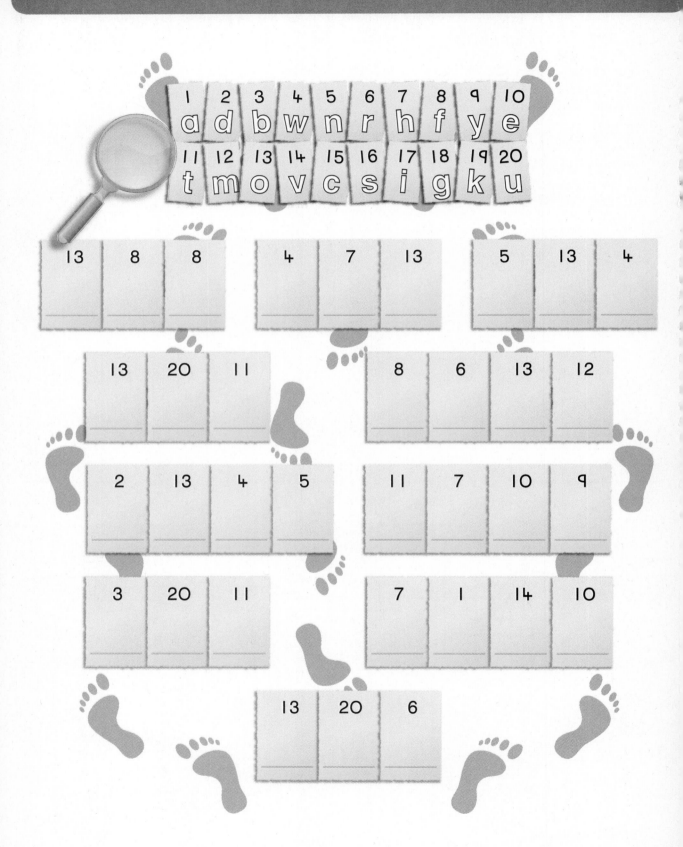

1	2	3	4	5	6	7	8	9	10
a	d	b	w	n	r	h	f	y	e

11	12	13	14	15	16	17	18	19	20
t	m	o	v	c	s	i	g	k	u

13 8 8 _____
4 7 13 _____
5 13 4 _____

13 20 11 _____
8 6 13 12 _____

2 13 4 5 _____
11 7 10 9 _____

3 20 11 _____
7 1 14 10 _____

13 20 6 _____

Learning Goal: Read, write, and respond accordingly.

94

Draw a car that can fly in the box below.

Write about your flying car.

 A GREAT CANADIAN WORKBOOK

CONGRATULATIONS!

This is to certify that

_____
Name

has completed Grade One English!

Date: _____

Aa Bb Cc Dd Ee Ff Gg
Hh Ii Jj Kk Ll Mm Nn
Oo Pp Qq Rr Ss Tt Uu
Vv Ww Xx Yy Zz